CONTENTS

Hellhole Hop

Well, here we are
in sunny Greece.
Can you feel the heat?
Do you dig the peace?
Back in the past
it was always like this.
Imagine that -
the world was bliss.

Tony Mitton

GREAT GREEK MYTH RAPS

Illustrated by Martin Chatterton

ORCHARD BOOKS

To Keith Gray and Laura Bailey
T.M.

ORCHARD BOOKS
96 Leonard Street, London, EC2A 4XD
Orchard Books Australia
Unit 31/56 O'Riordan Street, Alexandria, NSW 2015
First published in Great Britain in 2001
First paperback edition 2002
Text © Tony Mitton 2001
Illustrations © Martin Chatterton 2001
The rights of Tony Mitton to be identified as the author
and Martin Chatterton as the illustrator of this work
have been asserted by them in accordance with the
Copyright, Designs and Patents Act, 1988.
A CIP catalogue record for this book is available
from the British Library.
ISBN 1 84121 805 7 (hardback)
ISBN 1 84121 807 3 (paperback)
1 3 5 7 9 10 8 6 4 2 (hardback)
1 3 5 7 9 10 8 6 4 2 (paperback)
Printed in Great Britain

But something happened
to turn things round.
The whole thing started
under the ground.
Below the Earth,
the old Greeks said,
was a guy called Hades,
King of the Dead.

He was tall and dark
with a lonely frown,
and his face was pale
for he lived deep down.

His palace was a kind
of cave-hotel
for the souls of the dead -
some called it *hell*.
Now, one day Hades
was sitting when - *oof!* -
a great big chunk
dropped down from the roof.

It landed - *kerflump!* -
on Hades' head,
so he sent for his chariot
and sternly said,

I'd better go up
to the land of light
to check my kingdom's
roof is all right.

So he drove up above
with a rumbly sound,
then he took a little cruise
just to have a look around.

He stopped for a rest
in the cool of the shade,
and there he saw
a sweet young maid.

She was picking flowers
to put in her hair,
and she looked so fine,
yes, she looked so fair,
that he thought, "She's the prettiest
girl I've seen.
I'm gonna have to take her
to be my queen."

He didn't try to smile
or say, "Hello…"
or even call, "Hi, I'm
Hades. Yo!"

He simply hoicked her
up in the air.
"Hey!" she cried out,
"That's not fair!
That's no way
to ask for a date.
Who taught you
your manners, mate?"

Then she took in the chariot,
spooky and black.

But Hades gave
his dark horse rein
as the chariot tore
across the plain
till they came to a river
too deep to cross.
Hades thundered,
"Ready, hoss…?"

He cracked his whip.
It lashed the ground.
And a cleft appeared
with a roaring sound.
The horse flew down.
The chariot followed.
And soon the whole
darn lot were swallowed.

On they went,
down a deep, dark pit,
till the chariot stopped
and that was it.

Hades helped
the girl get down.
Then he looked at her
with his long, dark frown.

"I am Hades,
King of the Dead.
You'll be my queen
when we've been wed.
But first we need
to break the ice.
Tell me your name,
and I'll be nice."

The young girl thought,
"This guy is mad.
He's old enough
to be my dad.
But as he's a king
I must stay calm.
I'll use my wits
and lots of charm.

It just won't help
to scream and shout.
I'll wait for Mum
to bail me out."

"My name," she said,
"is Per-se-pho-ne.
But mostly folks
just call me 'P'.
I am the daughter
of Demeter.
No one tries
to fool or cheat her.

She's the goddess
who makes things grow
and helps the crops
to flourish, so,
if you don't put me
back in place
there *will* be trouble -
watch this space…"

But Hades' mind
was firmly set.
"Persephone,
my little pet,
I want you to be
my Underworld Queen,
so back on Earth
you'll not be seen.

I'll make arrangements
for the day.
We'll soon be married,
come what may!"

Well, that was it.
And, up above,
Demeter raged
at Hades' love,
at how that mean old
King of Shade
had snatched away
her darling maid.

And she went bonkers,
off her head.
"OK!" she shrieked,
"I'll give you *dead!*"

She went to Zeus,
the highest god,
and gave his chest
a hefty prod.

"I'll make plants wither,
fade and dry.
And then all things
on Earth will die.
So then there won't
be any food.
You get my meaning?
Eat that, dude!"

And just to show
her threat was real,
she made the world
begin to feel
what it was like
when tough Demeter
turned the dial down
on her heater.

Alas, the Greeks,
they were undone.
Till then they'd only
known the sun!
The leaves turned brown.
The folk turned blue.
And what could any-
body do?

It seemed the world
was at its end.
Poor Zeus was driven
round the bend.
"Hades!" he yelled,
"Give up the girl.
The world is in
a crazy whirl.
Just see she gets back
to her mum.
Or else, I fear,
the end has come."

But Hades crooned,
"Don't hold your breath.
You think that *I'm*
afraid of death?

And furthermore,
I ain't no fool.
You know full well
that there's a rule.
Whoever eats
in Hades' hall
can never leave
this place at all.

"My gardener gave
the girl a treat,
a pomegranate,
ripe to eat.
And maybe just
to be polite,
Persephone took
a tiny bite.

She only swallowed
three small seeds.
But that's enough
to serve my needs.
The girl is mine.
She stays with me.
So drop the matter.
Let it be."

24

Demeter wouldn't
let this go.
She brought on frost
and ice and snow.
She brought on all
of winter's blight.
The gods could see
the poor world's plight.

"If we don't fix this
soon," they said,
"the world's a goner,
wasted, dead!"

They called a meeting
on their mount
to try and settle
this account.
Hades was there,
Persephone too,
and fierce Demeter,
in a stew.

At first they argued
bitterly,
but Zeus broke in
with, "Now hear me!"

He took a breath
and rolled his eyes,
then started, "Right,
it's this way, guys.

Nine months, Persephone,
she stays
and helps her ma,
Demeter, raise
the things that make
Earth sweet and green.
Then, after that,
she'll not be seen.

"The next three months
she'll spend below.
For those, to Hades
she will go.
And while she's gone,
her ma will cry,
and growing things
will seem to die.

This plan will happen
every year,
a season scheme
that's neat and clear.
Now, that's my verdict,"
boomed the god,
and gave them all
a final nod.

Persephone gave
her ma a kiss.
Then what she said
to her was this:
"Don't worry, Mum,
and don't feel mad.
Three months in twelve
is not so bad.

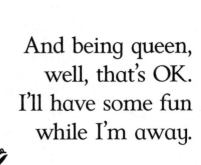

And being queen,
well, that's OK.
I'll have some fun
while I'm away.

Old Hades may look
cold as ice.
But actually,
he's rather nice.
And - *hey!* - his palace
down below
looks great for clubbing,
doncha know?

So while you're shivering up here, I'll be in my disco gear, down below in Hades' cave grooving through that winter rave.

"At last!" cried Zeus.
"So that's OK!
Go, Hades, fix
your wedding day.
But while you're down there
with young P,
remember just
how cold we'll be!"

Apple Race Rap

Listen to me, folks.
Did you know
that dating was different
long ago?

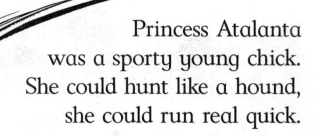

Princess Atalanta
was a sporty young chick.
She could hunt like a hound,
she could run real quick.

She didn't pick flowers
or sew with thread.
She was off with the hunt
which she often led.

So when she had to marry
to please her old dad,
the thought of it just about
drove her mad.
"OK," she sneered,

'Cos when it came to running,
she was the best,
and there weren't any men
who could pass *that* test.

But Princess Atalanta
was a beautiful prize,
and she wouldn't go short
of hopeful guys.

So she added, "If he wins,
then I'm happy to wed.
But if he loses,
he ends up dead.
(And the winning post
will wear his head!)"

Well, guys showed up
just to try at the race,
and the gory winning post
wore many a face.

But one fine morning
a prince dropped by,
and a single look at him
made Atalanta sigh,
"Now here's one time
I'd like to be beat.
But I can't change the rules
and I'm not allowed to cheat.

I just don't think
I could stand it - *oh heck!* -
if *that* handsome head
came off at the neck."

She needn't have worried
so much for this man,
'cos he knew the score
and he'd come with a plan.
He'd prayed to Aphrodite,
down on his knees,

I love Atalanta,
so help me, oh please!

Now, fair Aphrodite
was the goddess of love,
so she'd come straight down
from Olympus above,
saying, "Real, true love
is precious and rare,
and yours sounds strong
so I'll help you there.

"Take these apples,
one, two and three,
they're golden and magic
and lovely to see.

Each time you roll one
in front of her eyes,
she'll let out a gasp
and stop in surprise.
Atalanta's fit
and she runs real fast.
But each time she stops
you can speed on past."

Now, when it was time
for the race to begin,
the princess looked sad
so he shot her a grin.
Then at the word "*Go!*"
they were off down the track.
She was ahead,
but he wasn't far back.

He rolled the first apple
in front of her feet.
"Ooh!" cried Atalanta,
"Isn't that neat!"

She bent down to get it.
The prince went by.
So then to catch up
she had to try, try, try...

But as she overtook him,
he threw down another.
Atalanta saw it
and shrieked,

The prince panted on
to the finishing line.

The princess made ground,
she was ready to pass,
when down dropped the final
fruit on the grass.
It gleamed so golden.
It shone like the sun.
And as she stopped to get it -
phew! - the prince won!

Aphrodite smiled.
Cupid shot his darts.
And that race ended
with two happy hearts.

So if you wanna pick yourself
a partner that's cute,
ask Aphrodite
for some of that fruit!

RAP RHYMES
by Tony Mitton
Illustrated by Martin Chatterton

Collect all the books in this award-winning series!

❏ 1 Royal Raps	ISBN 1 86039 366 7	£3.99
❏ 2 Big Bad Raps	ISBN 1 86039 365 9	£3.99
❏ 3 Fangtastic Raps	ISBN 1 86039 881 2	£3.99
❏ 4 Monster Raps	ISBN 1 86039 882 0	£3.99
❏ 5 Scary Raps	ISBN 1 84121 153 2	£3.99
❏ 6 Robin Hood Raps	ISBN 1 84121 157 5	£3.99

Look out for these Greek Myth Raps!

❏ 1 Mega Greek Myth Raps	ISBN 1 84121 803 0	£3.99
❏ 2 Groovy Greek Hero Raps	ISBN 1 84121 799 9	£3.99
❏ 3 Mighty Greek Myth Raps	ISBN 1 84121 811 1	£3.99
❏ 4 Great Greek Myth Raps	ISBN 1 84121 807 3	£3.99

Rap Rhymes are available from all good bookshops,
or can be ordered direct from the publisher:
Orchard Books, PO BOX 29, Douglas IM99 1BQ
Credit card orders please telephone 01624 836000 or fax 01624 837033
or e-mail: bookshop@enterprise.net for details.

To order please quote title, author and ISBN
and your full name and address.
Cheques and postal orders should be made payable to 'Bookpost plc'.
Postage and packing is FREE within the UK
(overseas customers should add £1.00 per book).

Prices and availability are subject to change.